EVERYDAY VILLANELLES

Everyday
Villanelles

Kevin Arnold

fmsbw

San Francisco, California

ISBN 979-8-9921594-4-8

Cover artwork by Joshua Rampage

Author photo by Monika Rose

fmsbw

San Francisco, California

CONTENTS

FOREWORD

In 1975, after realizing they used the same approach to breaking creative blocks, musician/producer Brian Eno and artist Peter Schmidt collaborated on a deck of cards containing simple aphorisms or prompts to encourage lateral thinking. These often-gnomic *Oblique Strategies* have become a go-to inspiration for poets, composers, painters, filmmakers, etc. There's an edgy cool factor to this cultural phenomenon, which the centuries-old French verse form known as the villanelle can't claim. Nonetheless, Kevin Arnold's embrace of the challenging technique illustrates that, though the villanelle's strict approach may seem quaint, it's an equally powerful tool to drive lateral thinking.

The villanelle's dynamism lies in forced constraint. Even a brief description of their mechanics can make villanelles seem dauntingly rigid. Over nineteen lines, the poet must conceive of five tercets followed by a final quatrain. Two repeating rhymes and two refrains are the glue that holds together the whole. These strictures force the imagination to push for ever more innovative ways to achieve the pattern without devolving into or relying upon easy or familiar ways to stick to the landing. Test yourself by thinking of rhymes for "love," "light," or "sky." It doesn't take long before one begins to feel burdened by the risk of cliché. At this juncture, lateral thinking must shift into overdrive and bushwhack toward a less conventional solution.

The result is that content grasps the reins and the poet is pressed to excavate unexpected imagery, emotion, perspective, or insight from a realm far below the surface "thinking" mind. The forcing function of form unearths freshness. It's at this point that the repeating lines take on disruptive power. Repetition and rhyme work at a more limbic level and allow for a reunion of the intellectual with the emotional, a harmony that T.S. Elliot noted had been missing since the Metaphysical Poets of the 16th and 17th centuries, when he referred to a "dissociation of sensibility."

The poet and reader may both feel more at ease with, connected to, and regenerated by the dance through which a villanelle leads us. Kevin Arnold has titled this collection *Everyday Villanelles*, perhaps to inoculate us against intimidation or the kind of analysis I've employed. Please don't let my philosophizing about the alchemical properties of the form spoil your everyday delight.

Tamsin Spencer Smith
San Francisco, CA

INTRODUCTION

All my previous poems have been "free verse;" with no repeated lines and little rhyme. But I counted among my very favorite poems two villanelles: Dylan Thomas's "Do Not Go Gently into That Good Night," and Elizabeth Bishop's "One Art." Those two poems kept tapping at my shoulder.

Their form included two lines that are repeated four times, including the first and third lines, and also constitute the last two lines. I started thinking of those two lines as a villanelle's magic couplet. I decided to try my hand at the form. Since then, when I have an idea for a new poem I attempt to compose a magic couplet. If I fail, I move on. But, more often than not, I find a couplet and expand it into the villanelle form.

To move beyond the magic couplet, I must insert a second line between the two couplet lines. This will establish another rhyme scheme, which must also afford adequate rhyming possibilities.

On good days a poem seems to grow organically to contain a theme and often a *volta*, a change, which expand the poem before returning home with the repetition of the last two lines.

I'm rigorous about following the repeating-line and rhyme scheme; my biggest variance from traditional villanelles is that, rather than larger pastoral or dramatic scenes, I attempt to focus on smaller situations, often with themes from everyday life.

Kevin Arnold
Palo Alto, CA

CLIMBING THE VILLANELLE

If you want to write a villanelle, it's a climb
Like any journey, the toughest part is to begin
Begin by pairing two good lines that rhyme

Those lines repeat four times, like a chime
Yes, that repetition can get under your skin
Especially toward the top of your climb

Organic growth can only happen over time
As rhyming drives you toward the looney bin
But you must re-work them all into rhyme

Slowly, you'll re-create the villanelle paradigm
It's worth it when new discoveries bring a grin
You knew all along a villanelle is a long climb

It can be most frustrating—it's not a pastime
As it finds its design, you'll get your pleasure then
Nineteen lines, and every single one must rhyme

Let your heart take over, make your head resign
You'll need a pencil with an eraser, not a pen
If you want to construct a villanelle, it's a climb
Begin by pairing two good lines that rhyme.

DEATH CERTIFICATE

You'll learn of them soon enough if your spouse dies
Every insurance company and bank want one
On the surface, they're what their name implies

A single page to document your spouse's demise
A midlife wedding, fifteen years, and now it's done
You'll learn of them soon enough if your spouse dies

They're surprisingly like the title to a car one buys
Or a salvage certificate, when, later, the car is undone
On the surface, they're what their name implies

The funeral home gives you several copies—a surprise
Proving there was a loving person and now there's none
You'll learn of them soon enough if your spouse dies

What do they say of a guy who, out of nowhere, cries?
Opposite of a birth certificate, when a new life has begun
On the surface, they're just what their name implies

Who'd think a piece of paper would bring tears to my eyes
What it says is last year I had a wife and now I have none
You'll learn of them soon enough if your spouse dies
Though, on the surface, they're just what their name implies

2

GERALD AYRES, WHO LOVED TO CALL ME CUZ

Gerry was assistant head of Columbia Studios at twenty-eight
Bounding from Yale to Hollywood with immediate success
Since he started a family, we all assumed he was straight

My family loved his visits from New Haven, no idea of his fate
There was something larger than life about him I'd profess
Gerry was assistant head of Columbia studios at twenty-eight

The man's success in Hollywood would be hard to overstate
He ran Columbia before finding other ways to progress
Married to warm Annie. Father of two. Assumably straight

He produced his own films, which were considered first-rate
Nominated and won awards—a great talent he did possess
After helping run Columbia studios at twenty-eight

Then he left Annie—it was men he wanted to date and mate
On one of his sets the star hugged me. Jodie Foster, no less
He married a man, after we all assumed he was straight

I didn't accept him as he was; I'm not proud I acted with hate
Ghosting him after he left Annie—that pain I could not bless
Gerry was assistant head of Columbia Studios at twenty-eight
Since he started a family, we all assumed he was straight

THINGS THAT WILL BE GONE

How my eyeballs fit inside my head
How briefly lust and love coexist
What will be gone when I am dead

Galloping uphill on a thoroughbred
Unhooking a bra with a one-hand twist
How my eyeballs feel in my head

At thirty named a department head
Moments with women I've kissed
What will be gone when I am dead

My first house, my first homestead
Where I was finally proud to exist
How my eyeballs fit into my head

The great writers whom I have read
Reading T. S. Eliot to my grandkids
Scenes will disappear when I am dead

The incredible things my kids said
Many pleasures not in this short list
How my eyeballs feel in my head
What will be gone when I am dead

TO KISS THE WAR GOODBYE

Eisenstadt's "The Kiss" wasn't created by any design
A svelte dental assistant and some random Navy guy
Holding each other in Times Square, near the big sign

His embrace of a stranger, the assent of her spine
Her strange, absolute assurance she had to comply
Turned the moment into flesh with no planned design.

Perhaps their uniforms gave them permission to align
Thrilling male and female onlookers and passers-by
Who, too celebrated the joy of victory near the big sign

Their passion, driven by the moment, seems genuine
With Japan's surrender, their country got to certify
A victory. "VJ" was tomorrow's newspaper headline

To accommodate him she contorts her back to entwine
Merging with a random warrior to kiss the war goodbye
Joining an entire nation's celebration near the big sign

Their country's success was the underlying story line
Leading the world by means that continued to mystify
Eisenstadt's "The Kiss" wasn't created by any design
A spontaneous embrace so near our nation's big sign

UNEXPECTED VISITORS

Galway may be dead, but he visited me last night
He'd been given a new poem and invited me in
Sharon Olds was helping too, already in the fight

It came in awkward blocks that had to be set right
They hoped new blood would get them going again
Galway may be dead, but he visited me last night

The heavy blocks made it very difficult to rewrite
The three of us, moving them, made an awful din
Sharon Olds was helping too, already in the fight

The space with the blocks was cramped and tight
It was awkward but we slowly made sense of them
Galway may be dead, but he visited me last night

I was so proud when I provided a little insight
These two who'd taught me poetry way back when
Sharon Olds was helping too, already in the fight

They appreciated my help with this strange re-write
Together, we three accomplished a surprising win
Galway may be dead, but he visited me last night
Sharon Olds was helping too, already in the fight

ALWAYS EIGHT

It's my voice at eight years old I keep hearing
I acted like things were fine, no help called for
When the kids were mean to me and everything

Long before any thoughts of God or worshiping
Perhaps it was because I felt uncared-for
It's my voice at eight years old I keep hearing

I've always kept it to myself, no bellyaching
"And everything" meant more problems in store
When the kids were mean to me and everything

That repetitive voice has been a steadying thing
It's background, it hardly bothers me anymore
My voice at eight years old I keep hearing

A lifetime later, I still hear that voice ring
It's a quiet voice, the opposite of a narcissist's roar
From when the kids were mean to me and everything

I can't imagine this voice ever disappearing
It's part of me—I don't want to lose it anymore
That voice of me at eight years old I keep hearing
When the kids were mean to me and everything

A LITTLE SLEAZE

Tree's roots reach out for other trees
I'll double down—they're lustful, too
They seem like a tease on her knees

Viewing trees as sexy might displease
Experts, who deny it's in their purview
Their roots reach out for other trees

True, not every forester or arborist agrees
Trees are pure, from their point of view
Ignoring those who tease on their knees

I'm asserting a peeping Tom's expertise
Regarding the wild things they pursue
As their roots reach out for other trees

Don't ignore the naked truth one sees
I've dug up roots, I've followed through
And know a few who tease on their knees

Illicit liaisons they seek, a little sleaze
I wish the experts would admit it's true
Tree's roots grab out for other trees
Precisely like a tease on her knees

AT THE DENTIST

They say it starts with a kiss but that's not true
Any look that promises more attention on the way
A seemingly random hint of availability will do

Women know many novel ways to imbue
Willingness, promises of something risqué
They say it starts with a kiss but that's not true

My dental assistant, using her mirror to view
Pressed her left breast in my right ear one day
And then her right breast into my left ear too

She used such pressure I mistook this for a clue
I tried to kiss her, but she turned the other way
Her hint of availability was a big misconstrue

Buttons undone allow clandestine peek-a-boo
If done well, hidden behind a feigned naivete
They say it starts with a kiss but that's not true

Kisses usually come in a subsequent rendezvous
Neediness confused me at the dentist's that day
They say it starts with a kiss but that's never true
Any seemingly random hint of availability will do

IT STARTS WITH JOY

Most writers feel joy in creating art
Dashing off a draft with all they've got
Fewer are attracted to the harder part

That first draft comes from the heart
Not from analytic rational thought
That's a lot of the joy in creating art

Critical dissection is the drudgery part
The crafty things that can be taught
That make us admit we're not so smart

As our initial vision is taken apart
It could be unreliable as a granny knot
Though it gives the joy of creating art

Still, there's a thrill in getting a start
Before grasping that your story has no plot
Or whatever you learn from the harder part

Brave souls take what's there and restart
Some give up, so their work comes to naught
But most writers feed such joy in creating art
That they knuckle down to the harder part

ONE GOOD LINE

In writing from the heart, I don't have much
But about horses I came up with this one line
"What they know best they know by touch"

It seems to be true for all mammals and such
Be it a horse, man, woman, or porcupine
In writing from the heart, I don't have much

It's true in a bear's den or a rabbit's hutch
Or for a human's friendly canine or feline
"What they know best they know by touch"

Pray it doesn't sound like Pennsylvania Dutch
A linguistic limitation, not my heart's decline
Though it's quite true I don't have much

Don't jam in a second-rate word like nonesuch
After my one good line it's best not to whine
"What they know best they know by touch"

Don't ruin a good canvas by trying to retouch
My one line is true, and I'm proud it's mine
In writing from the heart, I don't have much
But what I know best, I know by touch

SACRED TEXTS

We know Matthew, Mark, Luke, and John
To whom many genuflect and say Amen
Nothing by Mary, Rosalinda, or Yvonne

It doesn't seem different with the Koran
Might have been even more patriarchal then
Names like Abraham and Moses before John

In almost all sacred texts you'll come upon
God is He—has been since time knows when
No names like Mary, Rosellen, or Yvonne

Want "Petticoat governance?" Aww, c'mon
It's a man's world and always has been
Think of Matthew, Mark, Luke, and John

Stephanie's a lot less likely than Stephan
No Alexandria, Linda, Susanne, or Gwen
Nothing sacred by Melinda, Suzi, or Yvonne

There should be no surprise in the denouement
When our texts are from roosters, not one hen
And we know Matthew, Mark, Luke, and John
But nothing by Mary, Rosalinda, or Yvonne

EIGHTY YEARS AFTER D-DAY

To re-take Europe took American know-how
And thousands of Americans dying in France
Europeans are asking where's America now?

England would have fallen too, most avow
As Hitler employed his continent-wide dance
To re-take Europe took American know-how

More than one French woman became a *Hausfrau*
Of course, today is a very different circumstance
But Europeans still ask where's America now?

Decades-old alliances have disappeared somehow
Past the *Maginot Line*, he went *manse* by *manse*
To re-take Europe took American know-how

Our representatives now seem to disavow
Leader of the Free World? Not a chance.
Europeans are asking where's America now?

They ask who made up those slogans anyhow
World safe for Democracy? Not a second glance
To re-take Europe took American know-how
Many Europeans now ask where's America now?

CONSEQUENCES

I dropped French in the middle of my second year
My ear loved the sounds, but I didn't practice at all
I started my lifelong habit of failing to persevere

A language wasn't required, so I had nothing to fear
Instead, at five foot eight, I tried out for basketball
Dropping French in the middle of my second year

The consequences of dropping it were never that clear
Until later, when Paris sang to me with its clarion call
And I began to question my habit of failing to persevere

In the cafés, as strange words bounced off my ear
I regretted that I hadn't found the wherewithal
Three years after I'd dropped French in my second year

Unable to converse, I was a gauche conventioneer
As I mumbled "*Je ne sais pas,*" like a neanderthal
A result of my lifelong habit of failing to persevere

Unless I was spending money, I'd not even get a sneer
On that trip I took in the time of Charles de Gaulle
After I dropped out in the middle of my second year
A result of my lifelong habit of failing to persevere

WHERE YOU'LL END UP

If you dare travel, near home or far
You face this incontrovertible fact
Wherever you go, there you are.

A nameless nebbish or a rock star
On a journey precise or inexact
If you dare travel, nearby or far

After saying *ta-ta* or *au revoir*
The universe has a simple contract
Wherever you go, there you are.

Fly over Africa to Madagascar
This isn't the slightest bit abstract
If you dare travel, nearby or far

Whether by foot, spaceship, or car
Be you greeted warmly or attacked
Wherever you go, there you are

Visiting the next room or a distant star
Every destination shares this pact
If you dare travel, near home or far
Wherever you go, there you are

STAND UP STRAIGHT

"Don't slouch like an old man," I say
to myself, and "don't fall down,"
slightly more wary every day.

"Stand up straight," a posture to convey
a strong chap who won't let you down—
"Don't slouch like an old man," I say.

Falling is one place I've made headway
—I watch where I'll touch the ground—
even though slightly more wary every day.

My friends' minds begin to give way—
or rely on walkers—balance breaks down.
"Don't slouch like an old man," I say.

And I lose things, just carelessly mislay
keys and phones and where I am in town,
which explains why I'm more wary every day.

Weary of each compounding birthday,
I no longer play singles or ski—slowed down.
"Don't slouch like an old man," I say,
slightly more wary every day.

GONE IS GONE

As the pleasures of life are slowly withdrawn
The calls for dalliances, danger, and speed
Fall silent one by one as dark comes on

Thoughts of the final curtain being drawn
Lessen even the kneejerk wish to succeed
As the pleasures of life are slowly withdrawn

Sexual conquest is no longer a sine qua non
Even my readiness is far from guaranteed
And falls quiet, even silent as dark comes on

Still I have reasons to welcome each new dawn
And ample routines and pills—more than I need
As the pleasures of life are slowly withdrawn

I can be sharp as a tack or such a moron
While the loud chatter of my desires recedes
Falling silent one by one as dark comes on

What's done is done, what's gone is gone
I smile quite broadly at how little I need
As the pleasures of life are slowly withdrawn
And fall silent one by one as dark comes on

CATECHISM

My horse must see the power of God in me
Bearing carrot or whip or anything in between
She doesn't share the 'free will' given to me

Sandy and I are also God-made, like a tree
She's middle aged for a horse, not yet a teen
Sandy must see the power of God in me

We're not just concepts, each of is an actuality
Sandy can move, but more subject to routine
Tree has even less of this 'free will' given to me

But Sandy has more freedom than a tree
Still, there's no way for 'free will' to intervene
My horse must see the power of God in me

With free will, I can ignore God or be a devotee
Find some shoulder of a God on which to lean
That's this overwhelming 'free will' given to me

Should I mistreat my horse, God will see
In God's eye each and every action is seen
My horse must see the power of God in me
She doesn't share the 'free will' given to me

SURRENDER TO SLEEP

To get a good night's sleep you must give up the fight
Liminal is that vague state between awake and at rest
If you're still doing battle, you'll toss and turn all night

Reassure yourself you've not only the need but the right
Begin the laying down of arms as you get undressed
To get a good night's sleep you must give up the fight

Don't cross your limbs, and you can't sleep uptight
You've no chance of rest if you your mind is distressed
If you're still doing battle, you'll toss and turn all night

You can control your life by breathing just right
Inhale   Exhale   Repeat   Breathe from your chest
To get a good night's sleep you must give up the fight

Some artists find that liminal state a good place to write
Control your breathing and by sleep you'll be blessed
If you're still doing battle, you'll toss and turn all night

If you're victorious the next thing you'll see is daylight
Inhale   Exhale   Repeat from deep in your breast
To get a good night's sleep you must give up the fight
If you're still fighting, you'll toss and turn all night

AT MY DESK ON A SATURDAY MORNING

The local courts are wet, no mixed doubles today
I'm left to play with words, arrange a certain flow
Hoping that the muses do not lead me astray

I've learned writing requires some plugging away
I'd like to transcend like Henry David Thoreau
The local courts are wet, no mixed doubles today

With Saturday morning tennis I like to swing away
I hope a tried-and-true form will release that flow
The muses, goddesses all, will not lead me astray

I'd rather be hitting a crosscourt this spring day
Or slamming down an overhead with extra gusto
The local courts are wet, no mixed doubles today

It's wonderful you write poems, people never say
They'd rather comment on my serve or tennis elbow
No way those seductive muses would lead me astray

My missed doubles match haunts me all day
As I exchanged words for the tennis I had to forego
The local courts were wet, no mixed doubles today
Let's pray the muses do not lead me astray

TO THE NORTH, SOUTH, EAST, AND WEST

From the Bible, it's Job and Moses I know best
Still, "no Gods but me" I've wanted to outgrow
Lakota pray to the North, South, East, and West

North, winter, and the ways we're repressed
Whether to conform as before or finally let go
From the Bible, it's Job and Moses I know best

South brings comfort of Earth's nurturing breast
When the sun shines from South relax in its glow
Say your prayers to the North, South, East, and West

East, where sun comes up, is where we're blessed
Listen to God—what changes should we undergo
From the Bible, it's Job and Moses I know best

West, the source of water, where the sun finds rest
We can accept our passing with the water and its flow
Ending prayers to the North, South, East, and West

These are from the Lakota, who've been dispossessed
Let us not lose what they learned from nature long ago
From the Bible, it's Job and Moses I know best
But I also pray to the North, South, East, and West

PRUFROCK

"For decisions and revisions which a minute will reverse"
Says Prufrock just after "In a minute there is time"
The long line I think of as the very best in verse

Those nine words reflect my vulnerability to this universe
I save or spend or copulate and try to make it rhyme
For decisions and revisions which a minute will reverse

I often say them under my breath, part hope, part curse
I repeat Prufrock's lines all day, from dawn to bedtime
The long line I think of as the very best in verse

I believe in God—this isn't all just random or worse
I've never heard a rational contradictory paradigm
For decisions and revisions which a minute will reverse

Eliot's lines don't include one word to which I'm averse
They keep going off in my head, a familiar chime,
The long line that might be the very best in verse

I'm called an eternal optimist, which some think perverse
Compared to T. S. Eliot, I'm probably not worth a dime
For decisions and revisions which a minute will reverse
The long line I think of as the very best in verse

SCOTT AND ERNEST

The rich are different from you and me
Said Fitzgerald said to his friend Hemingway
Yes, Scott, he said, they have more money

I'm in Atherton, the richest place in the country
Up in hills near the reservoir on a sunny day
The rich are very different from you and me

Such elbowroom up here—I feel carefree
These houses cost over twenty million they say
Yes, Scott, they have more money

Although I'm a writer I've been around you see
worked for high-tech startups in their heyday
The rich are very different from you and me

I'm sort of a millionaire myself, theoretically
if you ignore my debts, a cynic might say
Yes, Scott, they have more money

Birds in these huge trees sing attractively
Look over there, stunning views of the bay
The rich are very different from you and me
Yes, Scott, said Ernest, they have more money

SCAMMED

I fell for a scam on the Internet
I thought I was talking to Xfinity
Everyday transactions pose a threat

I can't clear my mind, can't forget
It was in the bounds of feasibility
I fell for a scam on the Internet

They promised me a free headset
I never questioned their viability
Daily life is now a constant threat

No hint or reason to get me upset
I filled in secret codes with rapidity
Falling for a scam on the Internet

Now all my codes are on the dark net
I can't believe my own gullibility
Everyday transactions pose a threat

I must cancel three cards before I forget
Ignore another blow to my dignity
I fell for a scam on the Internet
Every new day brings another threat

A POET'S PRESCIENCE

Levertov told us to stop this show
She saw no way for the earth to last
She didn't want us to let the planet go

This was forty years ago
We had to do something fast
It was up to us to stop this show

Now, as reservoirs dry up or overflow
We've put mother nature in the past
Denise asked us to stop this show

A growing Arctic Archipelago
Rate of change is unsurpassed
She called on us to stop this show

She begged us to buck the status quo
Before we saw hurricanes lambast
She didn't want us to let the planet go

Even then, her words wove sorrow
While somehow remaining steadfast
Levertov pressed us to stop the show
Alas, we're still letting our planet go

CURTAIN CALL

I dread the starting of the fall
Preceding winter with its snow
Summer, come do a curtain call

Winter's such a long cold haul
Bone-chilling winds that blow
This awful starting of the fall

Winter months pass in a crawl
My often-green fields lie fallow
Summer come do a curtain call

Calm my fears, make them small
A brief respite from winter's woe
Before this starting of the fall

One sunny week I'll be good to go
It truly could be once and for all
Couldn't you manage a curtain call

Even two days on my patio
Prepare me for this long haul
I hate the starting of the fall
Summer, come do a curtain call

TOES IN THE SAND

Whenever things get too boring or bland
—sometimes I stare blankly at my shoe—
I wiggle my toes; pretend I'm in the sand.

Once, at trial, I did it on the witness stand
—the judge and jury, of course, never knew—
what I did when it was all too boring or bland.

It can be a reaction to people I can't stand
—even with them I have to come through—
so I pretend to wiggle my toes in the sand.

I know none of them would ever understand
—I don't toe-wiggle with people I look up to—
only when someone is too boring or bland.

It's not enough to fiddle with my watchband
or stare at the idiots who surround me, it's true,
I wiggle my toes; pretend I'm in the sand.

Or ogle a woman who takes me to dreamland
—thinking of a desert island with just us two.
Whenever things get too boring or bland
I wiggle my toes; pretend I'm in the sand.

VIVE LA DIFFERENCE

The difference between poetry and prose
is poems' naked space at the end of a line—
Prose wears armor, poetry no underclothes

Poems are gardens, novels great meadows
—neither brassiere nor panties to confine—
Such differences between poetry and prose

Poems always worry about what they show
—way more than bra-straps and pantyline—
prose wears armor, poetry no underclothes.

Poetry has far less space to be verbose
—it has to be frugal. It must live in the line—
A major difference between poetry and prose.

Early poetry was often sung, history shows
—Rhyme aided memory, words to enshrine—
Prose wears armor, poetry no underclothes

Each form works toward the other's shadows
—prose poems and poetic novels are fine—
Vive la différence between poetry and prose
Prose wears armor, poetry no underclothes

EARLY MORNING

She says "get up we have to get you fed"
I'm half asleep but there is light outside
This woman I'm living with, the redhead

I have to go to exercise—I'll do as she said
Most of our needs seem to coincide
She says "get up we have to get you fed"

I'm not perfect—I don't just pop out of bed
If she thinks I'm cold, she'll lay by my side
The woman I'm living with, this redhead.

I have prurient thoughts which I leave unsaid
As she hugs my back while I'm bleary-eyed
She, who said she wanted to get me fed

Should I get a little grabby, could she be led
To a moment of passion with me astride
This woman I'm living with, this redhead

I'm on the edge, so much left unsaid
Feeling her rub against my backside
Who said "get up we have to get you fed"
This woman I'm living with, the redhead

STALLIONS

Stallions are strong but don't fully submit
Said a horsewoman who always rode a mare
A new filly on the farm and they lose it

Male horses lose their way lickety-split
She felt safer on mares, "who take such care"
Stallions are strong but don't fully submit

She loved that mares never throw a fit
While males, even gelded, sniff the air
A new filly on the farm and they lose it

She smiled when she dropped this tidbit
Hinting male minds wander here and there
Stallions are strong but don't fully submit

Geldings and mares are aware of the bit
But stallions can go full-on devil-may-care
A new filly on the farm and they lose it

She knew stallions could never fully commit
After she saw one coupling with a mare
Stallions are strong but don't fully submit
A new filly on the farm and they lose it

DID IT HAPPEN THAT WAY?

It's mainly a question in nonfiction and memoir
If a spouse announces divorce in the ski lift line
Can you say their talk happened in a gondola car?

This thing they call me-fiction is the new superstar
Truth counts there, too, but is not the bottom line
Most talk of truthfulness is in class on memoir

In newspapers, truth is often buried in a sidebar
To describe how politicians whine and dine
There's no way to say it happened in a gondola car!

For space travel, if you want to visit a far-off star
Conjuring spaceships requires hints of their design
It's mainly a question in nonfiction and memoir

Not even poets can wander from truth too far
Sometimes it's truth against rhyme in a difficult line
Can we move our conversation to the gondola car?

That covers about all of writing's wide repertoire
I did it by the required place, the seventeenth line
It's mainly a question in nonfiction and memoir
Go on, say he dropped the bomb in the gondola car

COURTING

Part of every romantic situation
I'm talking the real world here
Is the other's financial consideration

Handsome but poor causes vexation
When the bill comes is he cavalier
Is part of every romantic situation

His wallet, not her heart's palpitation
Whether he's a dog-walker or engineer
Impacts the financial consideration

As she quietly analyzes his vocation
He's sleuthing too, that seems clear
It's part of every romantic situation

He's doing a concurrent computation
Her car, what model and what year
A complex financial consideration

Each hope for the right combination
The ideal relationship is peer-to-peer
Part of every romantic situation
Is the other's financial consideration

MERETRICIOUS

There's a word for deceptively delicious
—it started as an adjective for a prostitute—
it's that ten-dollar word meretricious.

Feigning patriotism while being seditious
—pretending great wealth while destitute—
both ways to be deceptively delicious.

A cute little puppy who's in reality vicious
—who will bite its owner like a mad brute—
fits that ten-dollar word meretricious.

When I'm guilty I try to act unsuspicious
—a shark in a friendly dolphin suit—
Trying to appear deceptively delicious

An avid partisan who claims to be judicious
—a church Elder in a house of ill repute—
both fit that ten-dollar word meretricious

Sworn testimony that's in fact fictitious
—a paid decision-maker who is irresolute—
each demands a word for deceptively delicious,
it's that ten-dollar word, meretricious.

HOW IT WAS IN 1960

It was sixty-five years ago
Kennedy and Nixon seemed tied
The entire republic was aglow

Nixon's makeup highjacked the show
As the debates saw them collide
It was sixty-five long years ago

My father and I were toe-to-toe
He was rock-ribbed on Nixon's side
The entire republic was aglow

For me, Kennedy had the combo
Being well-spoken and honest-eyed
It was sixty-five years ago

The country envied Jackie's beau
Say no to socialism! Dad scried
The entire republic was aglow

The results came in to-and-fro
It took days to count and decide
It was sixty-five long years ago
The entire republic was aglow

HENRY JOHN DEUTSCHENDORF JUNIOR

I'm down at the beach in Aptos on Monterey Bay
It makes me think of John Denver's sad demise
A death ruled an accident, which I ponder to this day

He was told the name Deutschendorf would never play
And fell in love with Colorado, so Denver's no surprise
I think as I scan the beach in Aptos on Monterey Bay

John died flying off Lover's point on a clear sunny day
A life filled with sun, then clouds, and then he dies
A death ruled an accident, which I ponder to this day

Colorado named him Poet Laureate in his heyday
I find his lyrics moving, and sometimes quite wise
Lovely like the beach in Aptos on Monterey Bay

Thousands of hours piloting and ran out of gas they say
I'm a pilot, and that's suspect for anyone who flies
A death ruled an accident, which I ponder to this day

At fifty-three, the joy of his earlier lyrics gave way
His remains paddled in on a surfboard under blue skies
I sadly recall at the beach in Aptos on Monterey Bay
A death ruled an accident, which I ponder to this day

DAYDREAM

I rewrote reality yesterday, just to see
I was still a middle child born late in the war
Only in my dream Mom paid attention to me

Dad had confidence too—acted less lordly
Him losing his job had been hard to ignore
I abandoned reality yesterday, just to see

Whenever she passed out, I wanted to flee
To dream those problems away forevermore
Mom really seemed to pay attention to me

Our affluent suburb still seemed fancy-free
Us, impoverished at the grocery store
Yesterday I abandoned reality, just to see

Much to disremember, can anyone blame me
What would happen to this poor sophomore
Only in my dream Mom paid attention to me

The key to the dream was the loss of reality
Attempt to blot out, find a way to ignore
Abandoning reality yesterday just once, to see
And I loved how my mom paid attention to me

THE GREAT WALLENDA

Life is on the wire; the rest is just waiting
Said Wallenda, the high-wire artist, whose
Single-mindedness was so captivating

Wallenda's strength came from not complicating
His determination with other people's views
Life is on the wire; the rest is just waiting

Even climbing up to the wire I'd be vacillating
Knowing, on the wire, there can be no re-dos
Perhaps that was why he was so captivating

Some days I find Wallenda's line infuriating
Where did he find strength to just push through
That life is on the wire; the rest is just waiting

Without risk, there can be no creating
It's no wonder we can't resist the bold few
Whose single-mindedness we find captivating

My problem may be I'm too accommodating
Lacking the will to walk in those shoes
Life is on the wire; the rest is just waiting
Single-mindedness itself is captivating

DRESSING IN THE DARK

Each day is shorter than the day before
Squirrels have squirreled their nuts away
Getting up has become a major chore

I can't take a quick dip in the pool anymore
Or sport Hawaiian shirts, even on a Saturday
Each day is shorter than the day before

Dark and cold seem to be what's in store
Even yesterday was longer than today
Getting up is beginning to be a chore

I'll need energy summer never called for
Dressing in the dark fills me with dismay
Since June, each day's shorter than before

Fetch socks and gloves from the cellar drawer
File my memories of summer's days away
Waking in the dark makes dressing a chore

I'll take my mind off—start planning for
Family holidays, especially Christmas Day
Each day is shorter than the day before
Getting up has become a major chore

TWILIGHT

My doctor wants me caffeine free
Women notice me less than before
I never imagined how this would be

I flirt as before, but they ignore me
I'm just not in the game anymore
My doctor wants me caffeine free

I so miss being touched tenderly
As my daily routines become a chore
I never imagined how this would be

Halloween is when kids are set free
Expecting goods by a knock on my door
My doctor wants me caffeine free

Costumes like those you always see
Each gets a quarter, nothing more
I never envisioned how this would be

This twilight time I did not foresee
Pondering all I've decided before
My doctor wants me caffeine free
I never imagined how this would be

THE RAKE

"What were you thinking?" asks my head
Heart says, "I was so lonely that weekend."
Heart and head will bicker till I am dead

This was about me asking Sabrina to bed
"I do like you," she said, "But as a friend."
"What were you thinking?" asks my head

My head sees my heart as a knucklehead
Is desire all heart, no head, in the end?
Heart and head will bicker till I am dead

Head says, "Your cheeks turned bright red."
Admitting that desire is hard to defend
"Sabrina's too good for you," says my head

Heart says, "In my dreams I saw us in bed."
"I want her as much more than a friend."
Heart and head will bicker till I am dead

I wish I'd blown her a kiss instead
Now my dreams of Sabrina have to end
"What were you thinking?" asks my head
Heart and head will bicker till I am dead

JUDY COLLINS IN NINETEEN LINES

Judy Collins was to play piano in the orchestra pit
But quit the classical world for folk rock's sincerity
Her singing landed Judy smack dab in the thick of it

"When I Was a Girl in Colorado" is her latest hit
Written at eighty-two, a true show-biz rarity
Long after giving up the piano in the orchestra pit

An early song she wrote, "My Father," is a favorite
And the whales sing with her on "Farewell to Tarwathie"
She's remained center stage, smack dab in the thick of it

Judy gave Stephen Sondheim his biggest hit
As she drew people in with her voice's clarity
Once she'd abandoned piano in the orchestra pit

On stage and off, she and Steven Stills were close-knit
Crosby, Stills, and Nash sang "Judy Blue Eyes" adoringly
Joining her at center stage, smack dab in the thick of it

Giving up, she downed a bottle of pills before she made it
Thank God she threw the aspirin up and avoided catastrophe
Around this Irish lass trained for piano in the orchestra pit
Who ended up center stage, smack dab in the thick of it

MISSED MESSAGES

Julie, please just pick up the phone
Rather than email, text or tweet
Don't tie me to every device I own

My laptop's yet another millstone
I must check or feel incomplete
Julie, please just pick up the phone

When you say "but I texted you" I moan
Especially that day you couldn't meet
Don't tie me to every device I own.

A text to my watch I can't condone
Especially in bed, alone, in a sheet
Julie, please just pick up the phone

Remember that broker well-known
Texting tips before they were obsolete
His clients' slaves to devices they own

On crash day he left his iPhone at home
His clients got him kicked off the street
Julie, please just pick up the phone
Don't tie me to every device I own

JIMMY BUFFET'S SONG

Bewitched by "A Pirate Looks at Forty" long ago
The wannabe pirate felt life had passed him by
At forty he pictured the life he'd lived as a sideshow

As if a bigger life lay somewhere over the rainbow
But we had to empty the stands by letting one fly
Bewitched by "A Pirate Looks at Forty" long ago

If we're not dead at thirty-seven like Van Gogh
Must we give up when we're no longer spry
Accept the day-to-day lives we live as a sideshow

Even if we've known what's at stake from the get-go
And, disappointed, always play the contented guy
Bewitched by "A Pirate Looks at Forty" long ago

There might be something to the art of letting go
Some clever way that we don't even have to try
To acknowledge our day-to-day lives as a sideshow

When the angel of death has us in his crossbow
May we at least get to call our friends to say goodbye
Bewitched by "A Pirate Looks at Forty" long ago
Knowing our routine lives have been a sideshow

TULIP TREES LIVE TWO HUNDRED YEARS

Should I return, I say to people who ask me
What would I like to be when I re-appear
I'd like to come back as a flower on a Tulip Tree

Their name is Tulip Tree Magnolia, properly
With yellow or pink blossoms this time of year
When I return, I say to people who ask me

My main job would be to attract a honeybee
I wouldn't want to attract rapacious deer
I'd like to come back as a flower on a Tulip Tree

A network of roots and branches would feed me
And hundreds of leaves help me persevere
When I return, I reply to people who ask me

But it's the hummingbirds I love whirlingly
Not a deer gobbling me up, not shedding a tear
A yellow or pink flower on a Tulip Tree

If tired, the bird could sit on that branch's knee
But it's a whirring hummingbird I'd love to hear
Should I return, I say to people who ask me
I'd like to come back as a flower on a Tulip Tree

—
44

A WORD MECHANIC'S LAMENT

The car I despise working on is the villanelle
They ought to take them off the road
Take that rhyming couplet and go to hell

A clanging 'b rhyme' can be death's knell
Those 'a rhymes,' used so often, can corrode
The car I despise working on is the villanelle

Repetition makes their readers want to rebel
They grab tire irons, try to break the code
Take that rhyming couplet and go to hell

One bad rhyme can make an awful smell
When they come in half of them are towed
The car I despise working on is the villanelle

Last week I saw one self-destruct pell-mell
Overworked, I've seen others explode
Take that rhyming couplet and go to hell

If you own one, I'd recommend you sell
The form's way too old to carry the load
I refuse to work on one more villanelle
That rhyming couplet can go straight to hell

THE WEEK BETWEEN

This week between Christmas and New Year's Day
With the year ending, what I need to get through
What to ignore, maybe work on; what to throw away

For a deduction, I must make my donations by Friday
Small details, the things I've put off, I still need to get to
This week between Christmas and New Years Day

So much comes to a head—no time for delay
My son's car insurance requires looking into
What to ignore, maybe work on; what to throw away

Nothing's as absolute as death and taxes, they say
Is the bank open? There's a constant sense of déjà vu
In this week between Christmas and New Year's Day

With Christmas past, everything feels in disarray
Memories of an old girlfriend come from out of the blue
What to ignore, maybe work on; what to throw away

The tax year ends, and another friend died yesterday
Memorials are more frequent, last week there were two
This week between Christmas and New Year's Day
What to ignore, maybe work on; what to throw away

WRITING YOUR RUSTIC SONG

Villanelle is an ancient Italian word for rustic song
Two lines are repeated four times, it's bittersweet
And only two rhymes, exactly nineteen lines long

Repetitions soothe and keep things moving along
But can feel confining, constraining, and obsolete
Villanelle is an old Italian word for rustic song

See, that last line had to fit where it doesn't belong
The demanding form can take you off your beat
With its "a, b, a" rhyme scheme, nineteen lines long

To find your voice, you might take a chance on
Finding a magic couplet and the lines to complete
Villanelle is an Italian word for rustic song

Give it a try even though it's a lot to take on
The form can be vexing, but don't accept defeat
Only two rhymes, exactly nineteen lines long

Getting lost you may find where you truly belong
When you nail the quatrain you'll feel so complete
Villanelle is an ancient Italian word for rustic song
With only two rhymes, precisely nineteen lines long

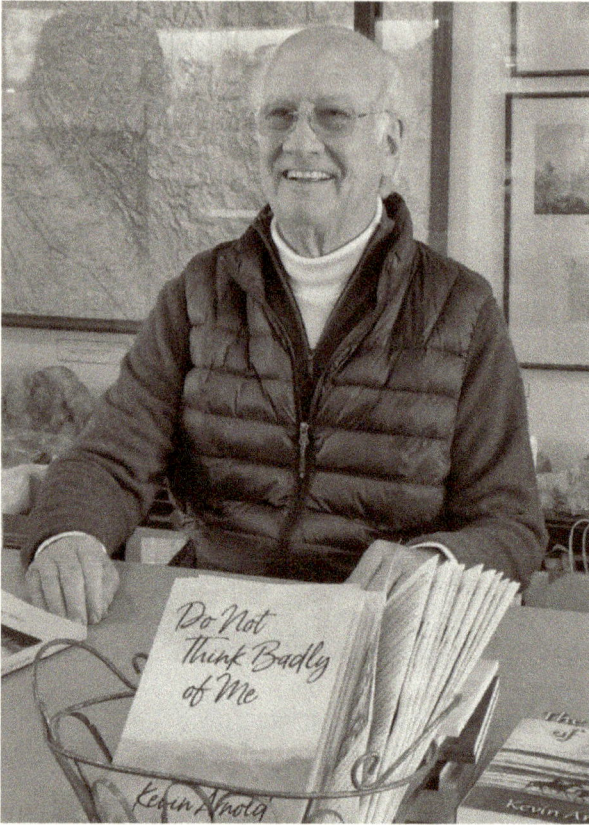

Kevin Arnold, 2022

Kevin Arnold was born in the Brooklyn Naval Yard during WWII, when his father served in the U.S. Navy. Arnold also served in the Navy, after graduating from the University of Wisconsin. He moved to Northern California at age 30 and earned an MFA from San Jose State University.

Arnold was President of the Poetry Center San Jose for thirteen years and helped start *Gold Rush Writers*, in the California foothills, where he's taught for fifteen years. The San Francisco / Peninsula California Writer's Club recently named him Writer of the Year.

Recent books include a novel, *The Sureness of Horses* (Manzanitas Writers Press, 2018), and a book of poems titled *Do Not Think Badly of Me* (Manzanitas Writers Press, 2022). Finishing Line Press published his chapbook, *Our True Song*, in the Spring of 2026. Arnold is currently working on a memoir to be titled, *Child of a Troubled House*.

THE PAGE POETS SERIES

THE DIVERS COLLECTION

Number 1
Hôtel des Étrangers, poems by Joachim Sartorius translated from German by Scott J. Thompson

Number 2
Making Art, a memoir by Mary Julia Klimenko

Number 3
XISLE, a novel by Tamsin Spencer Smith

Number 4
Famous Dogs of the Civil War, a novel by Ben Dunlap

Number 5
Now Let's See What You're Gonna Do, poetry by Katarina Gogou translated from Greek to English by A.S. with an introduction by Jack Hirschman

Number 6
Sunshine Bell / The Autobiography of a Genius, an annotated edition by Ben Dunlap

Number 7
The Profound M: found photos paired with poems by Tamsin Spencer Smith with an introduction by Matt Gonzalez

Number 8
The Glint in a Fox's Eye & Other Revelations, volume one of a three-part memoir by Ben Dunlap

Number 9
The Origins of Bliss, volume two of a three-part memoir by Ben Dunlap

www.ingramcontent.com/pod-product-compliance
Lightning Source LLC
Chambersburg PA
CBHW032057040426
42449CB00007B/1112